Sukoon: A Tryst Within

Suramay Pidara

BookLeaf Publishing

India | USA | UK

Made with ❤ on the BookLeaf Publishing Platform
www.bookleafpub.in
www.bookleafpub.com

Dedication

To the unwavering strength and ever-present joy in my life - My Parents,

To my mentor - Mr. Shyam Kodanda,

To the procrastinators, lovers, wanderers, and pure romantics,

To those who supported me in this journey and those that didn't,

Thank you for being my greatest teacher.

Preface

Sukoon (complete inner peace) is an ongoing emotional churning journey. This book is based on personal journeys and observations through the years. After many tumultuous battles, these musings led to a moment of peace.

I hope that in between these pieces, you find something with a place in your mind or heart where you can return to heal. So, for all the dreamers, warriors, and hustlers, this is for you and written with you in mind.

Writing this book was never easy; it took years of sifting through pieces to get here, especially finding unique translations for my Hindi/Urdu pieces. So, all of these are a lot of hard work, and I hope you guys can enjoy it with an open mind!

Acknowledgements

As someone who started with writing as a sheer expression of self, I was inspired by many people, events, and ideas around me. So a big thank you to them. My heartfelt gratitude to the BookLeaf publishing platform for making this dream possible and to all my future readers and editors.

Thank you to everyone who felt something in any of my pieces!

1. Ek Tijori

Ek band tijori ke sandook ki chaabi padi thi,
Kuch puraani aashayein usme seemit thi,
Kuch khushnuma, kuch bandagi bhari thi,
Jala kar unki raakh se nayi roshni nuraan hui abhi,
Shayad unke pinjado mai kuch kahaniya adhoor thi kahi,
Jinki daastan-e-aasmaan ki udaan poori abh hui.

Translation:

She left the key to old memories open,
And I took out all those wishes and desires,
Some half baked, some fulfilled,
They glowed with renewed vigor in the heavenly fire.
Entrapped in those ashes was my mind,
Which wanted to leave everything and everyone behind.
It flew from the bounds of its own limits,
and gave its shadows a good look one last time.

2. The Dying Soldier

Deep circles had engraved where his eyes used to
prevail.
His bones had been visually prominent right till his
spinal tail.
His hair had grown to become wires of his horrific
experience.
Shining with a lusty gray like the silver lining, as he
neared a molten strip of fence.
Now and then, a mist would arise comprising of
chemicals and Asian dirt,
and wipe off some of the blood from his torn and fleshy
t-shirt.
Those chemicals that he inhaled,
would force a cry from him,
that echoed in the middle of the desert.
The stars were absent from the charred and burnt sky,
and so were the people from the streets he passed by.
A few hours ago, the world had been familiar to him,
but then flashes of light, explosions of fire, and swift,
sequential, and speedy tornadoes left him grim.
To weariness, his body had started to surrender,
and in between the eeriness, he again started to wonder-
that all the militant groups had to fight because they had
to support their cause,

but they did not realize how terrible the state of the
country was.
His family was either dead or displaced,
and on the barren tracks of his cheeks, some tears now
raced.
With the name of God on his lips,
he gave way to the soul that freed itself from where it
had been cased.

3. I Will Wait For You

On the shores of sadness,
In the stream of happiness,
When the moon smiles in the sky,
I will wait for you.
When Hades comes to take me,
When the rain tears my eyes,
I will wait for you.
When I smile like an orange sun,
And through my eyes, your images run,
When my fate makes me fearsome,
I will wait for you.
when my heart beats faster than the drums,
in between the bottles of rum,
I will wait for you.
when loneliness pricks me like a pin,
when I think to love you is a sin,
When I write our names in the sands of time,
I will wait for you.
When my eyes become blood red,
and my body is anger-fed,
when my lips miss those sugar breath,
when my body is not covered by your warm sheath,
I will wait for you.
In my meaningless rhymes,

In my unfinished poems,
In my wordless songs,
I will wait for you.

4. I will wait for you too

Until waves twinkle in your reminisce,
and keep crashing
to the shores of my heart
and bring forth the memories of our first kiss,
I will wait for you too.
Until, with my love, you become luminescent,
my soul is intoxicated with your scent,
and in your love, I am proved innocent,
I will wait for you too.

Until on my door, death knocks,
as we seal our love on the bridge of locks,
and every inch of this fiery desire turns blue,
I will wait for you too,

The sun might heat my rage,
the world will feel like a cage,
the moon may turn my soul cold,
yet I won't feel young and bold,
because until my last breath, I will wait for you, too.

5. Addict

Ringing in my ears,
is her voice,
which brings me to tears,
with every noise .
When she is near,
My heart beats,
To watch her is a treat,
but to tell her is a fear.
Her chocolate eyes,
my mind needs,
her blonde hair,
smells like sweet air.
Her lips are like a pink rose ,
Which I want taste from close ,
the sun's drop at the crease,
Are a sight to please.
She swivels and serves,
deathly glares,
yet her honey dripped personality,
are just one of her flairs,
Our lives more woven than the fabric of life can knit,
She maybe the light, but I am her addict.

6. Waterfall

When I sit near a waterfall,
I think its beauty is, above all,
I hear its splashing sound,
and I smell its secrets spellbound.
Sitting here, I clear my mind,
And some fresh memories I bind,
Some peace here I find,
And all the sadness I leave behind.
When my mouth enriches with its taste,
The freshness in my body passed,
its purity relieves me of my sins,
and all of it is put aside in bins.
My heart goes singing about it,
I sit entranced thinking about it,
physically present,
mentally absent.

7. Partition

Am I lost in the abyss of cataclysm?
Is this the final gripping death's chasm?
The streets of my beloved city,
are filled with camouflage and ambiguity.
It was just yesterday when my shop was filled with
laughter.
My old father was arguing with the
customer about the price of a Pashmina,
Today I couldn't match the eyes of my daughter,
When she asked me 'Abu kya yeh hi Hota hai jeena?'
While I am cut off from my family and my country,
A man holding a rifle tells me-
That the government has abolished article 370,
And now Kashmir will be free.
I let out a nervous smile,
While I observe the deadening silence spread over a mile.
Hunger is gnawing on my existence,
But I will survive with persistence.
God has made me and all of us a fakir,
But we will all rise once again just like the Fir trees .

8. Too many storms?

A snake passes by,
the mind slithers,
A leaf drops nearby,
the mind withers.
Every inch of peace,
is turbulent here,
in every breath-
It feels like the end is near.
Speckles of ice,
feel like thorns of fire.
Each is pricklier than the other,
until there is no hope or desire.
Shards of memories,
are fragmented beyond repair,
and every ray of sunshine,
Brings a wave of despair.
The lines are blurred
between this outcast and the norms,
and it asks how many storms are too many storms.

9. Break Free

Lehere si utthi thi aur todna chahti thi uski deeware,
behena chahti thi wo udti fizaaon mai.
Par uske darmiyaan kuch rok raha tha ,
usse tod sa raha,
Kehna chahti thi wo ke haan usko yakeen hai,
par uska mann sawaalon ki chaadar odha tha.
Kya beshaq bekhauf hokar nahi apna sakti thi wo khud
ko,
todd nahi sakti thi kya wo saari bandhishein,
kya maloom nahi tha usse humaari chahato ki bekaraari,
Abh wo hai sirf apne khayaalo mai simti,
aur reh jaayegi humaari kahani adhoori.

Translation:
She desired to flow in the winds, gushing like Ganges,
She wanted to break free of all barriers of all ages,
Inner voices tamed her will, broke herself,
In a library of experiences, she remained secluded to a
shelf,
Would she never give herself a chance?
Will she never snap out of her trance?
When will she stop and get out of her thoughts?
O beloved! It feels like our journey here has stopped.

10. Mystic Feeling

Ek ahsaas sa tha
kuch khoya Jo kabhi na tha humara
humaara toh kya kabhi aaya nahi yaha
aaya toh kya uska gyan dhyaan bhi nahi tha
bas rooh mai ek kanta sa chubhe jaaye,
aur jiski bhanak bhi nahi mann usko hi bulaaye.

Translation:

This Mystic feeling
had me lose something that was never mine
It never even occurred to me
I had never even dreamt about it
yet like a prickly rose, it hurts my soul every day
and towards the shapeless, my mind finds a way
It wanders those dark alleys, those glorious days
yet it cannot find a sniff of the essence,
After a tireless search, it sits every night
on the streams of thought
hoping that one day it will take shape
and everything will make sense.

11. His Leela

Sansar se utth kar,
unki taraf mann jaane laga.
Ek peeda ka kichaav sa aaya.
Log badle, yug badle par hum nahi,
Hum apne chit ko saral karte gaye,
par phir bhi woh nahi dikhe.
Tabh laga ki shayad hum bhi unhi samsar ke jitna wo
humaara,
Shayad unka mann kiya
aur woh rach rahe hai ek nayi leela dobaara.

Translation:
Renouncing my world,
He brought me closer to reality.
But still, there was a pinging feeling,
Everything around me was changing, but not my mind.
For him, I was ready to leave it all behind.
I prayed and tried to see him, but to no avail,
When I opened my eyes, I saw his essence in every trail.
It felt like his presence had to say
That it was time for his creative play.

12. Blank Stares

Neither heroes nor villains,
they are just people with blank stares.
Illumined by a mirage of deceptions
are the souls behind these empty glares.
They wake up to the same sound
and find the same lack of zeal around.
Occasionally, their souls are lit up by a raging fire
and fills them with passion and desire.
It breaks them out of a trance,
And for once, they want to take a stance.
For once, they want to fly instead of fight,
they want to revert to the just and proper.
They want to be a right note in Bach's verse,
and immerse their soul into the flow of the universe.
They want to be a breath of fresh air,
And plunge out of death and despair.
In a city of serpents,
they set off to seek a gem's glow,
on their way, they are bit and torn to pieces,
And their journey suffers a deathly blow.
Then the sky falls on them
and crushes the aspirations that had put them at the
helm.

So now they climb up the same stairs-
and walk with those same blank stares.

13. Bliss of Solitude

Away from two faced diabolical devils,
that spit out words bitter as cud.
Masked with the veil of laughter,
Hiding their charred and blackened souls.
Away from all the hypocrites,
who act like Socrates,
but think like pennywise.
There is a paradise,
Where my thoughts roams,
into regions free of narrow domestic walls,
free from the beckoning death and heavenly calls.
Where angels from heaven,
reside in a merry harmony,
where all races are notes of a perfect symphony.
There is a world where love gushes,
from the walls of my heart,
and in its beauty, it pours it blushes.
There is a world free from apparitions-
of the society,
Where every human is worshipped as deity.
There is a world free from judgmental eyes,
Free from the problems of our own devise.
There is a world free from the divisions of every latitude,
This world is my bliss of solitude.

14. Journey

Λ mountain of experiences,
a sea full of chances,
awaited my arrival to the world of mortals,
where I could learn new values and morals.
As I moved forward, In the ocean of life,
There were gates through which I could not enter,
There were topics on which my opinions had to differ.
I walked on the lighted up streets,
on the edge of darkness.
I walked on the lanes of fires,
to keep me from falling into pits of desires.
Surrounded by earthly beings,
I saw some wonderful sightings.
My work struck many with awe,
but the orthodox said that I was always breaking the law.
Many hailed me as the best of our clan,
many wanted to become my true fan,
but as I reached the end of my road,
there were two stairs that flowed,
one that promised me all the pleasures that I didn't
enjoy,
and another that promised me real joy.
I wanted to think wise,
like a person who plays chess,

But ultimately I listened to my heart,
without thinking about its end and start,
and ascended on the stairs
that offered me true happiness.

15. Flickering Light of Hope

Silent melodies of melancholy,
blown out in puffs of smoke;

were enough to destroy the aspirations-
of a dreamy-eyed bloke.

He was too lost in his reveries-
to grow and blossom.

Like a birch tree's leaves falling in autumn,
he fell from grace and hit rock bottom.

He still cherishes-
the memories of his experiences.

However, in bottles of rum and grievances,
he slowly perishes.
Yet, he holds on to a loosening rope.

He still extinguishes darkness-
with the flickering light of hope.

16. Baap

Kuch nahi sunta, kuch nahi bolta,
shayad andar hi andar kholta hu.
Aulaado ki umeedo pe utra,
Pitro ki Jaagir se ubhra,
kabhi kabhi yehi sochta hu.
Ki jawaani ki mashaal kabh kamzor ho gayi,
kabh apni muskaan mereliye tazir ban gayi.
Kabhi Kabhi wo jhalakti si hai,
Jabh wo khilkihlaati si hai,
Par kya uski hasee bhi wohi jazbaa hai,
Ya fir kya mera humsafar bhi koch soch raha hai?
Saath chalte chalte bhi kyu alag se hogaye hai sabh,
Kya mukaam reh gaaya hai mera ye bas jaane wo rab.
Shayad apno keliye khud kho jaaunga,
Ek din phir apne aap se hi mil jaaunga,
Par baap hu na mai?
Mai kabh se sochne lega ke kya paaunga?

Translation:
Silence in my secrecy,
Solitude in my melancholy,
Born out of debt,
and carrying expectations,
Was all of this meant to be?

Did the flame tame too soon?

Did I smile too much too soon?

A glance of mine conveys this to her,

and her smile acknowledges that she infers,

In keeping everyone together, I am shared miles apart,

Brazen land runs over the rivers of my heart.

Someday they'll understand,

One day I'll find myself,

I'm a father, aren't I,

When did I start thinking about myself?

17. Mehek

Zindagi bezaar thi,
bas kamai aur rishto ka bazaar thi,
ek ahsaas laaya mand mand si chehek aur phir aayi uski
mahek.
Jabh woh aayi,
Khilhkilayi uski haasi,
Jaha humari aas thi phasi,
Hume laga ke shayad wo mann se judgayi,
Par phir wo mudgayi.
Kush choot sa raha tha,
samay beh sa raha tha,
oonchal ho raha tha wo lamha,
aur tabhi ussne palat kar dekha.
Abh jabh wo paas hai,
toh subah noor bankar uski palko par toot gayi,
par uske chehre se kal ki shyam dhali nahi,
mast aayi thi chehre pe par hasi wo bani nahi,
dariya abhi deewar todkar bahene waala tha,
mera humdum mujhse dil ki baat kehne waala tha,
par phir unko jaana pada aur wo chale gaye,
ay musafir hum intezaar mai khade rahe gaye.
pholo se khele uski zulfein,
Kai shararaton mai doobi hain,
apni hi ras mai dil pighlati,

apne hi saaz se sukoon laati hai.

Mai poochta hu musafir kyu ruka hai,

fir jawab mai hawa uske ahsaas ki mehek laati hai.

18. zulfein

Ajeeb khel hai tumhaari zulfon ka,
tumhari ungliyo se lipat kar,
auro ki nazaro se sharmati hai,
shayad yeh bachati hai apni haseen shararatein,
jiske noor ka guroor tumhe satati hain.

Aankhein noorani thi par nazar thi paini,
unki zulfoon nai kari aisi bechaini,
ke hosh mai woh sama gayi,
aur dil mai baith gayi wo maharani.

19. Khat

Log poochte hai ke tum unhe khat nahi likhte?
hum kehte hai zehen sejaaye tabh toh,
unse chand palo ki mulaaqat hoti thi,
fir sawaari pe nikal jaati hai wo shehzaadiyo ki tarah,
fir hum unki raha par simte rehte,
aur wo arso tak nahi dikhte,
jaane kyu phir log poochte hai ke tum unhe khat nahi
likhte?

20. Woh

kuch sochti hai woh
beparvah hai khayalo mai.
Duniya ki bandish se duur,
khushiyon ke makaano mai,
bepanah mohabbat ke naseeb mai woh khud likhi thi.
Phir kyu dhoondhti doosra koi unn khayalon mai?

Saumyata aankhon mai,
par sharar bhari muskaan,
kya har sheher kaa hota yehi bayaan,
ki leheraati hai zulfein teri,
jaise hawaa mai zaafran,
ithlaye tu jaise balkhata hua jahan,
kaise iss kudrat ke karishme pe khuda na ho meherbaan?

Iss duniyaa se kya matlab mujhe ay musafir,
jabh aapke jhumko ke shikar ho chuke hai,
unn aankhon ki masti ka kya tawajo,
jabh aapki surat ka nikhar ho chuke hai.
Abh tum baaz ho ya parinda, hume kya padi?
ho sakta hai mehengi pade ye dillagi,
par abh zehen mai tumhaare lafzo ka shikar ho chuke
hai.

21. Sukoon

Beheti chalti fizaaon mai,
Aaj kuch teher sa gaya hai.
ufaan laati iss samudri aandhi mai,
Aaj kuch tair sa gaya hai.
Tip tip karti baarish,
jaise behe jaaye sadak sahaare,
Mun mun karti tum,
jaise jaago mere kinaare,
Waise raango mai safaid sa,
Band mutthi mai tehri rait sa,
Kuch haath laga hai,
Jiske wajood se mai kuch nahi hu,
par milne par sabh kuch sa mahsoos hota hai.
Kya iss bante bigadte mausam mai khaalipan hai?
Yaa hain kuch banta hua sa makaam?
Ek nayi kiran ki umeed hai?
Yaa Kaal ki koi nayi reet hai?
Sukoon sa tha hai iss pal mai,
kuch sawaal sa hai iss hal mai?
Baaz aaj ek nayi udaan bharne ko hai,
Ay Musafir chal aaj fir koi nayi raha nikalne ko hai.